LOST
&
FOUND

Kenneth Clair
MacMillan

Suite 300 - 990 Fort St
Victoria, BC, Canada, V8V 3K2
www.friesenpress.com

Copyright © 2015 by Kenneth Clair MacMillan
First Edition — 2015

All rights reserved.

No part of this publication may be reproduced in any form, or by any means, electronic or mechanical, including photocopying, recording, or any information browsing, storage, or retrieval system, without permission in writing from the publisher.

ISBN
978-1-4602-5124-9 (Hardcover)
978-1-4602-5125-6 (Paperback)
978-1-4602-5126-3 (eBook)

1. History, Canada, Pre-Confederation (to 1867)

Distributed to the trade by The Ingram Book Company

Table of Contents

Prologue i
Bloomfield Station P.E.I. 1887 1
Albert County, New Brunswick 5
Toronto 1911 19
Calgary 1911 31
    I 31
    II 37
    III 40
    IV 44
    V 46
    VI 48
    VII 50
Toronto 1944 51
    I 51
    II 56
    III 58
Moncton 1944 61
    I 61
    II 63
Epilogue 69

LOST & FOUND

Prologue

As the nineteenth century was drawing to a close, several significant social shifts were occurring concurrently in Canada. Some affected all of the country, while some were regionalized; some were social-structural, while others were cultural.

The most significant change, which influenced the entire country, was the opening of the Western territories to settlement and the subsequent development of the Prairie Provinces; Manitoba, Alberta and Saskatchewan. The expansion of the railway system was both a "magnet" and a "means," enabling people to move to previously unheard-of locations. Thousands of people were drawn from other regions of Canada and from dozens of other countries, each seeking a future in the new land.

At the same time, another change was sweeping the country. The seeming success of the Confederation experiment, starting in 1864 but continuing through the early part of the twentieth century, encouraged many groups with widely divergent interests to consider "uniting" in the hope of establishing a collectively greater influence than they could muster individually. The rationale was that if union was possible for groups whose self-interest was as much at cross-purposes as were those of Upper Canada, Lower Canada, British Columbia, and the Maritime Provinces, any type of union was possible.

The rush toward church union by denominations that had little or nothing in common was a part of the consequence of that hubris.

Methodists of various stripes were pressured into uniting with one another. Presbyterians, noted for their congregational independence, were affected. Baptists, with persuasions almost as numerous as the number of their congregations, were feeling the draw — and the pressure — to unite into some denominational association.

By 1890, Methodism had coalesced into one main body and was, at the diocesan level, considering union with the mainstream of Presbyterianism and with the Anglican Church. When the Anglicans withdrew from union negotiations in 1891, their place was filled by the Congregationalist Church, which was intent on uniting with other groups as a strategy for institutional survival.

From 1890 onward, and especially after the departure of Anglicans from the Church Union movement, Methodism was afflicted with seriously divisive pressures. The hierarchy of clergy, especially the bishops in Ontario, was committed to forming a United Church, at any cost. Protests from the laity throughout the country and from the lower level clergy, especially in eastern Canada, went unheeded. The strategy adopted by the bishops to deal with the opposition was to replace anti-union clergy with more cooperative appointees.

By the turn of the century, tens of thousands of Methodists were so seriously disaffected by the politics of church union that they left the church, seeking either secular consolation, or spiritual consolation with newly emerging church organizations. Many individuals, drawn by opportunity or forced by circumstance to relocate, found themselves without a predictable church to attend in their new communities.

A denominational label was no longer an accurate predictor of the nature and quality of instruction or fellowship offered by a local church. A new resident in a community could attend a church whose denominational connection was familiar but whose method of worship, cultural values, and social mores were entirely unfamiliar. In the ensuing chaos, families were divided, individuals isolated, and children alienated.

The story that follows is the account of one such family. All of the people in the story are real people, who by one means or another found their way into the Church of the Nazarene. In a few instances I have changed their names to avoid embarrassment that their real identity might cause.

The opinions expressed by the characters in the story are those of the characters, not the author; they are pieced together from surviving documents of their day. They are certainly shaped and coloured by the political and social divisions of that time and should be understood as such.

The principal characters, Henry and Velma Adams, are a specific, real couple but I've enriched their experiences by including in their story a few elements from other people's histories. The intent is not to mislead but to exercise an author's prerogative in dealing with a basic fact of human life: very few people live far enough outside the mainstream of common human experience for their lives to make a good story. All people have a few interesting things happen to them but only a composite of persons, like Henry and Velma, can tell enough about life for the reader to grasp the essence of their time and place.

The events are all real, but they are not singular. The kinds of things which happen in this story happened again and again, to various people, in various places, at various times. We can't write about all of them for many of the people are no longer alive and most of them weren't aware that something of historic significance was happening to and through them. The records we do have; a few letters, a few stories, a remembrance here and there, are precious. They point to a way of church life that has almost entirely passed by.

I have collected my data and tried to write in such a way that Nazarenes now, entering our second century as a denomination, can feel what it was like to be part of our Church in its infancy. Henry and Velma's story could be the story of countless early Nazarenes, from countless rural places in Canada, who for a variety of reasons, moved to one city or another looking for an opportunity to build a life. In the process and in the alienation caused by their dislocation, they came in contact with other people of like mind, who shared a common need: to be loved and accepted as they found their way in the complex society of the twentieth century city.

Many of our early Nazarenes went full circle, later moving back to rural and small town Canada, taking with them the message of the Church of the Nazarene. That message is that God doesn't demand theological precociousness, or ecclesiastical sophistication of His people. He is willing to call any people "holy" who, in simple faith, claim their portion of His Holy Presence.

Clair MacMillan
Moncton, New Brunswick
May 1, 2014

Meet Henry and Velma ...

Bloomfield Station P.E.I. 1887

Six-year-old Henry Adams shivered in the March wind as he stood on the platform at the railway depot. He cringed against his father's leg in terror as the train drew near. The overwhelming noise and size of the engine had a double effect on him, both attracting and repelling him. He hid his eyes with his hands but couldn't resist the impulse to peek through his numb fingers at the approaching giant. His blue lips quivered as he quickly moved his hands from his eyes to his ears, trying to shut out the clanging of the bell and the harsh scream of steel against steel as the brakeman plied his trade. He barely heard the loud swoosh of the escaping steam but was gloriously enfolded in its sweet warmth as it swept over him and the biggest moving thing in his world settled to a sighing halt a mere three feet away. Every nerve in his body was on edge and the hair on the back of his neck stood straight up as he absorbed the total engulfing of his senses.

Transfixed by the entire experience, he hardly noticed as his grandfather and grandmother stepped tearfully forward to say their goodbyes. Walter and Emily, Henry's parents, returned the embraces, a little uncomfortable at the public display of affection, yet overcome with emotion at the significance of the parting. Henry, blissfully unaware of anything but the exciting prospect of actually riding on the train, hugged his grandparents dutifully, then turned with a whoop of delight to run to the passenger car.

To Henry, they were going for a ride on the train. For Walter and Emily, they were leaving the Island in search of a new life.

The economic depression on Prince Edward Island had become too much for the Adams family. The accustomed prosperity, which had seen the family holdings grow to more than three hundred acres, had waned in the face of the new trade treaties with "The States." When trade with Boston and New York had been negotiated through Charlottetown, the times had been good. But now, since the Island had joined confederation in '73, the scene had changed.

In Upper Canada, the seat of the federal government, the economy was booming but every Islander was convinced that Prince Edward Island was paying for it. Taxes, tariffs, transportation charges and surcharges, broker fees, and, worst of all, federal politicians' salaries, had cut farm profits by fifty-five percent. Prince Edward Island was in crisis.

To ease the strain, Walter, the eldest of nine children, had approached his father after the crops were in, the previous fall. At first, Waldron Adams resisted his son's suggestion that he leave the Island and buy a farm in New Brunswick. Things were bound to get better again, he insisted, when all the politics had run their course. His arguments, though, were perfunctory for they both realized that the situation would not improve quickly. Waldron Adams was a realist, and when Walter assured him that it was best to go, that he had "prayed-through on it," Waldron was at peace with the decision.

As Walter and Emily were leaving that day, after tearful good-byes at Bloomfield Station, Waldron slipped an envelope into Walter's pocket. "I've been putting it aside," he said, "to buy the old Gard farm when things improved. I was going to help set you and Emily up there on a place of your own. You've earned it and I give it with prayers for God's blessing on your future." It was three hundred and fifty dollars.

LOST & FOUND

There was no time to say any more, to protest, or to re-think any of the decisions that had led to this moment. The conductor's shout, "All 'board," the creak and whoosh of the steam engine preparing to depart, left no time: Walter, Emily and little Henry climbed on the train and headed for a new life on a farm near Moncton, New Brunswick.

Albert County, New Brunswick

THE FARM HAD seemed prosperous enough when Henry was a child, though ninety acres would never make anyone rich. There was fresh running water through the back pasture, the well was artesian and didn't need a pump in even the driest summer; the stand of two hundred mature sugar maple trees assured late winter cash-flow; the birch grove was a ready source of easy fuel wood. Not a bad arrangement for a small family with modest needs and tastes.

Old Isaiah Steeves had accepted Walter's two hundred dollars as down payment and agreed to take the remaining fifteen hundred in annual payments of two hundred dollars at minimal interest. They shook hands on the deal, went to the county registry office and signed the book. Eight years and sixteen hundred dollars later, Walter and Emily owned the property outright.

Those were eight wonderful years.

There was no Methodist Church in the community, so they began attending the Primitive Baptist Church just up the road. After three weeks they were totally confused. It seemed that the main subject for the "Primitives" in Sunday School, Morning Worship, Sunday night evangelistic service, and Wednesday night prayer meeting, was the high crimes and misdemeanours of the "Four Square Baptists" who worshiped just down the road. Walter had quipped to Emily, on the way home the last Sunday they attended, that if the "Four Squares" were that different from the "Primitives" they might not be all that bad.

Two Sundays with the "Four Square" church had proven only one thing: The two churches were mirror images of one another. Walter and Emily didn't return for a third Sunday.

The next week they went across the side road to the Reformed Baptist Church, hoping there would be time for prayer, praise, and worship. They weren't encouraged. They were greeted with a tirade against shopping in the city instead of the community general store, against the evils of the city where "the Catholics run the saloons and dance halls, and where the Anglicans and Methodists run the liquor stores and brothels."

Offended at the characterizations, Walter found himself longing for the encouraging, uplifting singing of the Bloomfield Methodist Church. He wrote to Pastor Hardy asking for a suggestion about where they could find a good church.

Pastor Hardy had written promptly, suggesting that they try Central Methodist in Moncton. A classmate of his from Mount Allison University was the pastor and Hardy was quite confident that they would feel at home there. After an hour's conversation about their spiritual needs and little Henry's emerging need for religious instruction, Walter and Emily decided to give it a try.

The following Sunday they hitched the mare to the surrey and made the four-mile journey into the city. They found themselves on the steps of Central Methodist just as Pastor Ashley arrived. He greeted them warmly, made a promise to speak with them after the services, and went to the platform.

Although the people were all strangers, and the sanctuary was more elaborate and elegant than anything he had ever imagined, Walter felt at home immediately. The songs stirred his religious memories from childhood and the service was reverent and uplifting. Pastor Ashley spoke authoritatively, yet kindly, about the merciful judgment of God. At the close of the service he invited inquirers to come into the adjacent room to discuss their spiritual needs with the pastor or one of the lay preachers.

Without even speaking to each other, Walter and Emily arose at the invitation and found their way to the inquiry room. True to his word, Pastor Ashley was the first to greet them there. He gently asked how he could help. They poured out their story, expressing their hunger for Methodist fellowship and worship, and their frustration at being too far away to find it in their own community.

After listening intently and offering prayer for their situation, Pastor Ashley made a promise. "If you can find two other families in your community who will gather with you in a Methodist Class Meeting, we will send a lay preacher once a month to give you leadership. You only need to take an offering to help pay for his expenses."

As they drove home, Walter and Emily were overjoyed. They would come to Central as often as they could, but between times they would work on getting a Methodist Class Meeting started in their own community.

The first part was a chore, but a happy one. They came to look forward not only to the services in Central Methodist, Moncton, but also to the ride to and from the city. Henry loved the weekly trip to Moncton and he absolutely adored his Sunday School teacher, Miss Lockhart. He learned to tell the stories from the Sunday School papers, prompted by the pictures. By the time he was eight he knew almost all the stories by heart.

On the Sundays when the weather was too bad to travel, Henry dug out the old lessons and papers and went through each one, confident that his teacher would mail this week's papers to him. He went to the postmaster in the general store on Wednesday afternoons and bravely asked if there was anything for him; there always was. But the delight in receiving the mail, great though it was, could never make up for missing the chance to be in class with his friends, in the loving care of Miss Lockhart.

The second task, that of putting together a class meeting, was much more daunting. No one in the community was interested in what the Methodists had to offer. This was hard-shell Baptist turf and every possible variety of Baptist opinion was represented in a community church. There were the before-mentioned Primitive, Four Square, and Reformed Baptist congregations within "a stone's throw" of each other, an apt figure of speech, so Walter mused, in light of their attitudes toward each other. Within the radius of another mile you would find the New Light Baptists, the Old Light Baptists, the newly formed Fundamental Baptists, the Freewill Baptists, the Pre-millennial Freewill Baptists, and the Church of Christ (Anabaptist.)

Down the way in Hillsborough, there was a similar array of choice; all in varying degrees of support or opposition to Hillsborough Baptist's initiative to develop a joint coalition under the title, "United Baptist." Walter, Emily and Henry had traveled the nine miles to Hillsborough several times, hoping to find some support for their Class, but none emerged; Hillsborough had its own Methodist Church.

Walter neither understood nor cared for the issues that gave each congregation its raison d'être. His efforts to find even one family to meet with him and Emily for spiritual nurture in their own community went unrewarded. In fact, they soon found themselves the target of gossip, about the only thing the "Battling Baptists" (a moniker tagged on them by the editor of the *Moncton Times*) could find to agree upon.

At times the gossip grew oppressive and even escalated to near persecution. Several times the customers of the General Store threatened to go to town to shop if the storekeeper insisted on buying Emily's butter and eggs. But for the most part it was merely the frostiness accorded to any outsiders who moved in and then failed to align themselves with one of the prevailing factions in a rural community.

Pastor Ashley went beyond his promise and did send a lay-preacher to visit them and pray with them each month, despite the absence of any other local support. And each year the pastor himself would come, accompanied by his pretty wife, to make a personal call. That was always a great day! For Walter, Emily and Henry, life was happy, even given their immigrant status in the community.

In 1895 their world collapsed.

The first blow was the news by telegraph that Walter's mother was seriously ill and not expected to live. She was, in fact, dead by the time the message got to Walter and Emily. They boarded the train in Moncton and traveled with sorrowing hearts to the ferry crossing, and then across the Northumberland Strait. Walter's brother, George, met them at the Borden train depot. As they rode together on the narrow-gauge rail line, first to Summerside, then on to Bloomfield, he told them sorrowfully that church life in Bloomfield had changed, and not for the better.

Pastor Hardy had moved to Souris, and the Bishop had appointed a man from Toronto as his replacement. Church services had changed dramatically. They no longer sang the familiar gospel songs; the new pastor read from some new-fangled city thing called *The Lectionary*. He read his prayers as if God was a stranger to him and all he ever preached about was the need to join with other churches to form a United Church. The only sin he ever mentioned was "disunity," though he had never explained where that sin appeared in the scriptures; and the only invitation he ever gave for people to pray was when he called them to say the Lord's Prayer. It was even rumoured that the new pastor was known to take a social drink or two in some situations. The Methodist Church was changing.

In his sorrow, Walter only nodded at the litany of George's complaints. At the funeral, he noticed the cold, formal attitude of the service and the strange, unfamiliar hymns. When the service closed without any direct reference to his beloved mother and her years of work in the Bloomfield Methodist Church, his heart began to burn with anger. For now the anger was not directed at God, but at this interloper in Pastor Hardy's pulpit. Church life would never be the same for Walter.

The second disaster occurred on Walter's return to Moncton, when Pastor Ashley resigned the Central Methodist Church, under pressure from the Bishop to promote the Church Union. Bishop Caldwell had announced his position at Conference that summer. At first he had been willing to engage in some discussion regarding the proposed union but as time passed, his position became intractable.

In November he had made his final statement clear. Any pastor who opposed Union would be well advised to seek assignment in another Conference. The Maritime Conference of the Methodist Church was on record as being in favour of the Union with the Presbyterians and Congregationalists. The Anglicans, because of recalcitrant priests, had dropped out of the negotiations — the Methodists would not fall prey to the same divisive spirit.

Pastor Ashley's resignation was quiet and gentlemanly:

"I will not," he said, "draw the people of God into controversy. I have been called to be a shepherd of the flock of God's children. I don't know everything there is to know but I do know that in my ordination I took a vow to obey my Bishop. He has given me two choices as a direction for my obedience. I choose to resign and quietly serve God where He will place me rather than vote for something my conscience cannot bear."

Central Methodist Church was outraged! The congregation struck a committee to have the Bishop censured but the action died, lacking the support of the pastor. The very day that Pastor Ashley vacated the manse and moved to California, sixty-one families signed a declaration that they would never enter Central Church again until the Bishop was removed. Walter and Emily did not sign, but they were devastated. This was the Church they loved; many of their friends had signed and the prospect of traveling four miles on Sunday to hear something like he had heard at his mother's funeral, left his heart cold and empty.

Pastor Ashley made one final trip out to the farm to see Walter and Emily. He encouraged them to not lose heart and not to grow bitter but trust the Lord and serve Him only. "How can we do that," Walter asked, "when we can't find a church here in our community, and when our church in the city has been stolen from us?" Pastor Ashley couldn't find an answer.

The final blow came just weeks later when Emily died in childbirth. Little Minnie lived only two days but everything that Walter had lived for died in those three days. He cried out to God repeatedly, begging Him to spare his wife and baby girl. He bargained, he pleaded, he promised everything he could imagine, but to no avail. When the sheet was pulled over Emily's face something in his soul was enshrouded too. It was never again uncovered in this world.

Henry tried his best to offer some consolation but it was as if his father didn't hear him. He tried quoting the Sunday School verses he had so faithfully memorized but Walter rebuffed him. His soul ached for his mother who was gone but even more for his father, who though still there physically, had somehow become absent too.

A few of the neighbours stopped by the day before the funeral to offer their sympathy. Henry tried to receive them graciously but Walter's sullen silence chilled the parlour more than the cold November air. When Mrs. Rosthay, Clerk of the Adventist Freewill Baptist Church, came in to opine that this is what comes of keeping company with those unruly Godless Methodists, Walter's silence broke and Henry cringed in the corner, overwhelmed by his father's rage. He had never seen him speak in anger before, say nothing of shouting at a woman.

The day of the funeral, the new pastor at Central Church, Mr. Downing, rushed into the sanctuary at the last minute, hardly even noticing the grieving father and son. The two coffins were placed at the front of the church, the little one in front of the bigger one. Mr. Downing asked the usher in a stage whisper, what were the names of the deceased and the next of kin. For all the difference it made to the ceremony he might just as well not have asked.

His words were eloquent enough, but neither Walter's nor Henry's ears were attuned to eloquence: they listened in vain for a mention of Emily's and little Minnie's names, for some personal word of hope and comfort. It never came. Mr. Downing didn't even greet them at the door following the service. He had to hurry away to a meeting with the mayor.

Walter lost interest in almost everything after that. He continued to work the farm, after a fashion, doing only the barest essentials to eke out a miserable existence. His anger grew darker each day as he blamed God for Emily's death and blamed the church for having promised that God cared anything for him.

Several times over the next few months, two of the lay-preachers from Central Church stopped in at the farm to say hello. Walter always greeted them civilly but without much enthusiasm. They asked if they could pray with him but Walter refused: God had let him down, and it was up to God to take the next step to heal the rift. Despite their pleading, Walter was immovable.

When the lay-preachers reported to Pastor Downing after the last visit, he seemed uninterested. His only response was that it was foolish to think that a layman could do a clergyman's job. The lay-preacher's program was disbanded shortly thereafter. Clergyman Downing could never seem to fit a visit into his schedule. Walter took up drinking to fill the void.

As they plodded along at subsistence level, Henry never went hungry but Walter never went thirsty either. They lived in the same house, shared in the same chores, and ate at the same table but

Walter neither encouraged nor participated in conversation. The shroud over his soul was permanent. Henry was alone.

When Henry turned sixteen he left home to work in the Intercolonial Railroad repair shops in Moncton. He never saw his father alive again. When he and Velma got married three years later, Henry made a special trip to the farm to ask his father to attend the ceremony. He couldn't find him anywhere around the farm. No one in the community could recall seeing him sober in recent months. Henry left a note, telling Walter the good news but Walter never responded.

Henry and Velma moved into a third-floor apartment on Lester Street and for the first time since his mother died, Henry felt that life could be happy again. The walk to work, straight up St. George Street, took twenty-one minutes, but the rooms were warm and the rent was cheap.

Velma's family attended First Baptist Church and Henry dutifully took up attendance with them. At times when they would enter on Sunday morning he would glance across Queen Street at Central Methodist, hoping and praying that he would see his father.

Often, as Pastor Phillips droned on in his sermon about the impending Baptist Union, Henry would daydream about the old days across the street with his mother and father. The services here at First Baptist were beautiful, the surroundings elegant, the deacons devout, and the congregation respectful and reverent, but his soul ached for something more. It was not a cry for the past, a little boy weeping for his childhood — it was an adult soul, broken and crushed on the merciless wheel of life, crying out for healing.

Walter died in 1901, on January 22nd, the same day that Queen Victoria died. No one ever knew exactly what happened. Some people speculated that he had gotten into some bad moonshine and in his stupor had fallen off the Gunningsville Bridge. Although the tide had been out, there was still enough water in the channel to put an end to Walter's mortal suffering.

The practice of medical science was still primitive enough for the coroner to be unsure about the exact cause of death. It might have been the fall from the bridge and the fracture in his skull; it might have been the water in which he was found, face down; but then again, it might have been the methyl alcohol he had imbibed two hours before. Each was, in its own right, sufficient cause for Walter's demise. The case was closed.

The old Methodist parson, who was supplying the pulpit since Mr. Downing had gone to Sackville to become Bishop, was gentle and kind at the funeral. Henry sensed, in a way he hadn't for a long time, that God was near. Even the denouncing of the manufacture and distribution of "the devil's brew," was stated in a way that evoked mercy for the victim rather than wrath for his weakness. Henry even dared to hope, as the funeral concluded, that God would understand Walter's last years and would extend that mercy personally to him.

Henry put the farm up for sale the next day, hoping to get enough money to buy one of the new houses out on the West edge of town. He sold the equipment and few chattels that anyone wanted, and was able to pay the back taxes. Walter hadn't left much of value behind. By the time Henry had cleared the balance at the general store and paid the undertaker and the clergyman, there was nothing left. In fact, he had to dig into his own meagre savings to pay the last forty-three dollars. Walter's affairs were finally in order.

The farm didn't sell. Months turned into years, shutters began to rot, and the orchard began to look like a jungle. Alders grew up around the lawn, choking out the view from the road. It was too depressing for Henry and Velma to even go and look at it. The first two years, they harvested the apples and took them home for preserves. It was nostalgic, but not worth the day's trip to get them.

In the Spring of 1905, Henry arranged for Headly Allain, one of the neighbours, to tap the maple trees on shares. That paid the taxes for three more years. The sugar was good, said Headly, but it was more work than it was worth for half a crop. He had enough of his own trees to tap.

Henry and Velma talked once or twice about moving out to the farm and beginning to work it themselves but they really had no heart for it; what's more, they were wise enough to recognize that neither of them had a head for it either. Where would they begin? She was, and always had been, a city girl. Walter had never bothered to tell Henry anything about farming. On mature second thought, they had concluded that though the pay wasn't great, the work at the Shops was steady and secure.

The overdue tax notices began to take on a nasty tone when Henry missed the second annual payment. By summer of 1910, the papers had been served and the eviction notice delivered. It irked Henry to no end that the sheriff had insisted that he be there to be evicted. Henry had protested that he hadn't lived there in fourteen years, that he had inherited the place and had no intention of fighting the tax seizure. But rules were rules, according to the sheriff. In Henry's mind it was nothing but an excuse to embarrass him. His disillusionment ripened to full maturity when he discovered that Headly Allain had bought the place from the government for the back taxes.

He broached the subject with Velma in the surrey on the way back to town. "The railroad is looking for experienced machinists in Upper Canada and on the Prairies," he began. "What would you say if I put in for a transfer? There are plenty of jobs in Toronto and Hamilton. And land and jobs are plentiful in Alberta. What do you say? We could try Toronto and if we don't like it we could move on west. We're young and strong. They say there's big money to be made for a hard worker."

Velma was hesitant at first. Several of their neighbours had been talking about going west but she had dismissed their idea as idle chatter. She couldn't imagine living any place other than Moncton. As an only child, she couldn't imagine leaving her parents alone. Although her grandparents, her aunts and uncles and cousins all lived close by she hated the thought of her parents aging without her. But before they climbed the stairs to their little apartment she agreed to think about it. In her mind she had said she would pray about it but given Henry's now apparent disinterest in religion, she said she'd "think."

The longer she prayed about it, the warmer she grew to the idea. Their life was going nowhere in Moncton. They were both almost twenty-nine years old. She looked toward the future with a dawning consciousness that they were already in a rut.

Her parents, hard-working immigrants from Germany, were still living in the rented house on Botsford Street that they had occupied since before she was born. Their dreams of owning their own place had long ago died. The prospect of Henry doing any better than her father had in "The Shops" was slim. Henry was a fully licensed machinist when he was twenty-five; her father had gained that honour at twenty-one. At twenty-five, her father was foreman; Henry, at twenty-eight and counting, had little prospect of promotion in the next decade, maybe two. The honour of being promoted was one thing, but the pay didn't make much difference. Both generations were wretchedly poor.

They talked it over again and again during the next few months. Velma hoped that Henry would just make the decision, one way or the other, and tell her what to do. Henry was equally uncertain. Throughout the following summer and fall they vacillated, one week coming to one decision, the next week, the opposite.

Finally, the following spring, after a long, serious talk with Velma's father, Henry was ready to make his decision.

Velma was ready with her answer:

"Whatever you think is best," were her words, but in her mind she quoted that beautiful sentiment from the book of Ruth, "Whither thou goest I will go." They left on the train for Toronto on Tuesday evening, April 11, 1911.

Toronto 1911

As they stepped onto Front Street from Union Station, the couple was assaulted, first with the noise, and then with the speed. They were dazed! Everything was so big, clamorous, and loud, and so fast that for a moment they were stuck in their tracks. They couldn't imagine how they could have made such a colossal mistake. Velma choked, burst into tears, and began to shake; Henry clutched her, hoping to reassure, but conveying instead his own speechless dread.

Directly in front of them a machine, more monstrous than they could have imagined, towered over a hole that had been dug for a foundation. Henry had heard of construction cranes but this was beyond belief. In the shops back home they had huge machines that lifted the boilers onto the engine running gear but in comparison to this they were like children's toys. Gazing upward to the top Henry found himself growing dizzy. He took Velma's arm and together they started across Front Street.

Moments earlier, the station agent had glanced quickly at Henry's Inter-colonial Railroad employee transfer documents and told him, abruptly, to report to the office on King Street to arrange temporary housing. Before Henry could ask where King Street was, the agent had scurried away to deal with some other issue.

They stood for several moments, trying to get oriented. Henry saw a bench in the distance and led Velma to it. When she was seated he went to the friendliest looking face he could find and asked directions to the King Street office. The young man was pleasant enough as he directed, "Go across Front Street after you go out the Station door. Go straight up Yonge Street three blocks to King. Turn left, and the third door on the left is what you're looking for. They'll fix you up with a place to stay."

Henry breathed a sigh of relief, thanked the young man, and started back toward Velma.

They arranged for their belongings to be placed in storage temporarily and then they stepped into the spectacle that they now beheld. Henry's memory flashed to the moment, years ago, when he had first accompanied his parents to Moncton. Standing beside Front Street now, he was overwhelmed with a sense of his smallness and felt like a little boy again. But now there was no mother or father to turn to for strength. He glanced to his left and seeing the fear in Velma's eyes, steeled himself for what lay ahead.

The rush of people — more people than they had ever seen, going in more directions than they had ever imagined, at a pace that left them breathless, was only the beginning. The street railway ran right down the middle of the roadway; two electric streetcars approached; one from each direction; each moving so swiftly that it couldn't possibly stop — apparently heading toward a disastrous collision.

Henry's railroader's mind prepared for the worst. He grabbed at Velma and tried to shield her from the inevitable rush of steam when the two train-like vehicles met. his heart was in his throat as the trolleys passed one another and squealed to their respective stops on opposite sides of Front Street. He had heard of electric streetcars but was unprepared for how different they were from anything in his previous experience. He glanced around sheepishly, hoping no one had taken note of his reaction. Velma had noticed but she, equally in awe, took it as a confirmation of the appropriateness of her own response.

They found their way to the Duncan Street apartment building and climbed the outside stair to the second floor tenement. Henry placed the key in the lock and they stepped inside. Their rooms on Lester Street back in Moncton had been small but this place made the memory of them seem palatial! Velma, away from the prying eyes of strangers, burst into tears, sobbing wretchedly into Henry's shoulder. "Can we go home; please Henry, let's forget it all and just go home. I can't bear it!"

The noise from the street below penetrated the walls and poured in from every crack and opening. A streetcar clanked by, its bell dinging as it approached the next stop; a baby in the next apartment was crying dismally, a door slammed below, a thousand strange and intrusive sounds encroached on the little space that was supposed to be their new home. Everything in Henry's heart agreed with Velma's plea but in a shallow, hoarse whisper he managed to croak out, "We have to give it a chance, dear. Let's try it for a few weeks."

Velma sat on one of the straight-backed chairs in the kitchen while Henry returned to the station to hire a teamster and his truck to bring their few possessions the eleven blocks over to their new residence. They didn't have much but two hours later when it was all installed in the three rooms amid the provided furnishings, it did start to take on some of the feeling of home.

The next morning being Saturday, they rose early to explore their new environs. They agreed that the two things they needed to find immediately were a grocer, for they would need to eat, and a church where they could worship and feed their souls the next day. The grocer turned out to be no problem. Just half a block down King Street, nestled among the larger buildings, was a tiny food market with bread, butter, eggs, vegetables, some fruit, lots of canned goods and, best of all, fresh meat.

The quest for a church was much more demanding. They asked the grocer but through his broken English they could only discover that he was Roman Catholic and was in the Spadina Parish. They decided to retrace their steps from the day before, back toward the center of the city. They walked East along King Street and when they reached Yonge Street, rather than heading back south toward the station, they turned left and walked north to Queen Street. To their delight, after they had taken a few steps, they noticed set well back from the street, a large beautifully kept stone church building on the North side of Queen Street. As they drew nearer, Henry's heart leapt for joy. The words on the sign, Metropolitan Methodist Church, gave a glimmer of possibility that they might have found what they were looking for. Each word in the name evoked a welcome familiarity. They would worship here tomorrow.

Heading back toward their apartment, they grew more adventurous and followed Queen back across Yonge, York, then Bay Streets, and on over toward Spadina Avenue. It was a pleasant April day, much warmer than Moncton had been just five days earlier. The fresh breeze from the South made them believe that there was water near by, though they had no idea how close. They were content to search out the neighbourhood and see what was to be seen.

They passed a little frame building, which looked something like a primitive church, boasting a hand-painted sign declaring, "Salvation Army." They had no idea what that was or meant and walked on. At the corner of Catherine Street, wedged tightly between two small hotels was another little church-like building, bearing the name Queen Street Mission. The whole area around the building seemed depressed, so Henry and Velma hurried on.

At Spadina Avenue they looked to the right, and a few blocks up saw a large stone church. Even from this distance they could read the word, "Presbyterian." They turned south, three blocks to King Street and headed back east, past the grocer's shop, to Duncan Street and their little apartment.

As Velma prepared their late afternoon tea, they discussed their adventure. Both of them had noticed that though they had met many people on the sidewalks as they walked, no one spoke to them, smiled, or even looked them in the face. Toronto people didn't seem very friendly, they agreed.

At ten-thirty-five on Sunday morning, they arrived at the corner of Queen and Yonge Streets to make their way the block-and-a-half to the Methodist Church for the eleven o'clock service. What met their eyes caused them to stop in absolute astonishment. Back in Moncton they had seen an automobile once or twice. Lawyer Keddy was reputed to have one, though the streets were hardly passable for its frequent use. In front of the Methodist Church here on Queen Street was a line of more automobiles than they had ever imagined there could be in the entire world.

Henry and Velma peered intently at the passengers who were descending from these marvellous shiny vehicles to the pavement below. The men were in top hats and long black coats; the women wore furs and carried umbrellas, though the sky was clear. They strolled casually up the broad stone walk to the church steps, as if they owned all of Upper Canada. Perhaps they did.

Henry, never before conscious of clothing fashion, looked down at the suit he had donned for church. He felt shabby and ashamed. How could he go in among people like that, looking like this? Velma, sensing his discomfort, did a quick self-assessment. Her dress and coat had been new last Easter; she remembered how pleased she had been with them and had actually felt a little rush of pride (for which she quickly repented) when she and Henry had entered First Baptist just thirteen months ago.

After a few moments of uncertainty, Henry spoke. "It's a Methodist Church. They shouldn't care what we're wearing. Let's go ahead in." He remembered enough of his Sunday School lessons from years before to bolster his confidence.

To their great relief no one paid any attention to them as they ascended the walk to the front steps. An usher greeted them warmly just inside the front door and gave them a sheet of paper with the words "Parish Notices" printed across the top. They had never seen such a thing before.

They scanned the auditorium as they entered and were greatly comforted that their apparel was not much different from that of many of the other worshipers. They relaxed and decided to trust the Lord to help them in these strange surroundings.

The service began promptly at eleven o'clock and finished promptly at noon. The hymns they sang were unfamiliar but the sermon was easy to listen to and somewhat comforting to the young strangers from New Brunswick. The format of the service, all in all, conveyed a sense of assurance to them.

As they headed back down Yonge Street, Henry and Velma compared impressions. Velma was shocked that the assistant minister who'd made the announcements had invited all the young people to attend a dance at the church the next Friday evening. Henry agreed that it was unusual but what surprised him most was the sermon title given in the Parish Notices for the service that evening. "A Sane and Balanced Look at the Brewer's Trade" was the title, and it was followed by a brief summary of the content.

> *"While we Methodists deplore the abuses that occur when people misuse liquor, we maintain our historical stance of moderation in all things. We encourage Methodists to resist the voices of those people who would banish the business of brewing and selling beer and ale. We must respect the financial investment that many good Methodists have in this important aspect of our province's economic health."*

As Henry read it his mind flashed back to his father and the wreckage of his life, which had been fueled by alcohol. Velma, though she had little similar experience, was equally uneasy. Her mother had been a founding member of the Baptist Women's Temperance Union that later merged with other similar organizations to form the Women's Christian Temperance Union. Her family, and most Baptists and Methodists back home were staunch teetotallers. Both Henry and Velma were disconcerted enough by the experience that they decided to search out another church to visit the next week.

Henry began work at the Spadina Yard the following Monday. He was sadly disappointed that though his hourly wage had been increased by five cents over what it had been in Moncton, his assignment was actually a demotion. From his Moncton job as lead-hand, reporting directly to the foreman, he was relegated here to maintenance, little more than the "grease-monkey" position he had been assigned when he started with the Company in Moncton at age sixteen. When he came home that evening, he and Velma did some serious calculations.

The five-cents premium Henry received over his Moncton hourly wage hardly covered the higher rent they paid for the apartment. Velma was still reeling from her day trip to the grocer's store. Food was so expensive that she'd actually had to put some items back when she realized how much everything cost. Never having been out of Moncton before, it had never occurred to them that while wages might be higher in Upper Canada, prices might also be. The hopes of a better opportunity for prosperity in Toronto seemed bleak. They began casting their eyes westward.

The following Sunday they grew more adventurous. Velma had met a woman from the second floor of the apartment building who recommended they try visiting a Baptist Church up in the Roxborough area. It was a streetcar ride away but definitely the church for young people. Dutifully, though with many anxieties,

Henry and Velma boarded the Spadina streetcar at King Street and went North to Bloor Street. From there it was one block over to Walmer Road, and five blocks North to the church. Velma was smitten immediately with its physical resemblance to her home church, First Baptist Moncton.

The resemblance ended there. In front were parked an equally formidable array of motorcars such as they had seen at Metropolitan Methodist last Sunday. What was even more amazing was the number of people their own age, some dressed very much like they were, who were exiting some of the cars and entering the church. These young couples chatted easily together, laughed together, and made small talk as they entered the church building. No one seemed to notice Henry and Velma for which they were thankful.

The service was cold, austere, and formal. The hymns were hard to follow, calculated more to challenge the choir than to uplift the worshipers, Henry thought to himself. The interim pastor was rigid and perfunctory in his speech. His mannerisms were awkward and forced. Although it was obvious that he would only be there while the congregation selected a new pastor, the impression was etched permanently on Henry's and Velma's minds. They did not return. Over the next few weeks they tried several more churches but found none that seemed to suit their needs.

Work went from bad to worse in the following weeks. Henry met many other workers in the various assignments he was given, but tended to avoid prolonged contact with them. Being the newest man on the crew, he always seemed to draw the most menial task; being the shyest man on the crew, he rarely grumbled.

Although he had expected that it would be a while before he would have a chance to demonstrate the skills he had developed during his years of apprenticeship, he was not prepared for the tedium of the following days. Throughout the summer and into the fall, chore followed chore, nothing ever bringing him closer to the real purpose of his move to Ontario.

Things came to a head in mid-September. Henry was sent out on a repair crew to attend to some rails that were out of line. He protested to the foreman that he was a licensed boiler-maker, not a common labourer. The response was disheartening: "You are whatever I say you are! Go there, or go home. Your choice!"

Henry went but throughout the day questioned despairingly whether he and Velma should go back to Moncton or think about going further west. He looked around at his fellow workers, most of whom were older than he was. He talked with several of them during their lunch break. As it turned out most of them were boiler-makers too, putting in their time waiting for an opening in the trade. One of them, a forty-six-year-old from Sydney, Nova Scotia, had been waiting for nine years. Promotions were few and the people who got them were usually from Upper-Canadian families, or the children of the managers.

When Henry got home he told Velma that he'd had enough. They talked it over and decided they would head to Alberta as soon as their temporary housing arrangements terminated. That meant they would stay in Toronto until the last week in October and then catch the Canadian Pacific line to Calgary. The next morning, Henry went to the office to enter his request for transfer. In her letter to her mother that night, Velma wrote:

> "We have decided to go on to the west. Henry thinks he will have much better prospects for advancing in his work there. We haven't found it comfortable to settle here in Toronto. It is a wonderful city; its beauty is breathtaking. We walked by Queen's Park last Saturday; you wouldn't believe how majestic it is. Everywhere you turn they are building something! If Henry were a carpenter there would be

endless opportunities for good work. But he has his heart set on continuing to work for the railroad.

We have met many friendly people since we came but can't say we have found any friends. If we could say we had made some friends it would be so much easier to stay. We had hoped that we would find a church where we would feel at home, where people would be available to become friends but that hasn't happened.

Our visit to Walmer Road Baptist Church seemed exciting at first; the building was so much like our church at home. But everyone had their own friends and we didn't seem to fit in. Metropolitan Methodist showed some promise when we visited. The only problem was that we were both uneasy with how worldly they seem to be. Would you believe they were having a dance in the church hall? . . . and were encouraging all the young people to attend!

But what really finished us was the minister's attitude that drinking alcohol is acceptable for Christians. After what happened to Henry's father and our family's opposition to the liquor trade, we just couldn't accept that."

Velma continued for several pages. As she sealed the envelope a tear dropped from her eye. It occurred to her that a move to Calgary might mean never seeing her mother again. The train trip was well over a week long. She cried herself to sleep that night after Henry had dozed off. She felt so far away from safety, from comfort and security.

When morning came she felt better. Henry was cheerful as he left for work, more cheerful, in fact, than he had been in weeks. Velma went down to the post office to send her letter, and on the way back encountered the neighbour who had suggested they try Walmer Road Baptist Church. The neighbour was friendly again but in a hurry to be on her way. Velma noticed that people were like that around there.

When she got back to the apartment, she began to pack up the boxes she had emptied such a short time earlier. To her surprise, she found she was actually anxious be on the way, now that the decision had been made. Would things be any better in Calgary? She could only hope and pray.

Calgary 1911

I

HENRY LOOKED OUT the coach window as the train pulled into the station in Calgary. The train was two days late because of weather-related delays. He and Velma were damp, cold, and tired. The Pullman Coach would have made a better trip but all the "Company Pass" would allow without extra cost was upper-lower berth accommodation. They discussed whether it was worth twenty-two dollars for the space but decided against it. They didn't know what faced them in Alberta but thought it best to save every penny they could. As it turned out, they decided, it would have been worth every red cent!

When Henry and Velma stepped off the train onto the uncovered platform, they felt as if they would be swept away in the wind-driven downpour. It was only a few steps into the depot but by the time they made those few steps they were drenched. It wasn't until they had actually entered the station that they turned around and looked to the west. The sight made them both gasp in amazement!

Dark clouds hung menacingly over the city, casting undulating shadows over every building that was visible from the station. But beyond the darkness they saw a sight that was forever etched in their minds. Only a mile or so to the west (Henry couldn't judge accurately because of the unfamiliar terrain) there was a clear dividing line where the storm ended — beyond that line the sun was blazing brightly and even further beyond that they caught sight of the mountains. The intervening storm shadow made the bright sunshine on the snow-covered peaks look as if they were glowing, soft, yet dazzlingly white, like a gas lantern.

At first glance, Velma thought the mountain range was a ridge of clouds mounding up, preparing another assault of wind and rain. It was only after she had gazed through the gloom hanging over the city for several moments that she realized what it was!

"Henry!" she exclaimed, "have you ever seen anything more amazing? It's raining now but you can actually see the sunshine moving this way!"

She was right. Slowly, almost imperceptibly, the line between the clouds and sunshine was moving toward them. They stood in rapt silence as the brightness inched its way toward them. In five minutes the line was at the edge of the city, some twenty blocks away; in ten minutes, as they stood on First Avenue, awaiting the arrival of the electric streetcar that would take them to their temporary apartment, the sun burst upon them with a warming radiance they hadn't felt in days. It was like a personal welcome to a new life!

The process of making temporary housing arrangements had been exactly the same as it had been in Toronto. They could stay in the company owned tenement on Fourth Street, just a few blocks from the station, until they could make more permanent arrangements on their own. Henry would report to work the following Monday and would receive his first pay a week from the following Friday.

They felt at home immediately in Calgary. Where Toronto had left them feeling like street waifs, lonely and unneeded, every street corner in Calgary seemed to beckon them, inviting them to step in and be part of the future. Where Toronto breathed complacent self-sufficiency, Calgary panted, as if to say, "Hurry! Help us!

We need you!" During Henry and Velma's first few days they had pangs of home-sickness and a vague longing for the stability they had left behind, but they never once thought of going back east.

They immediately began their search for a church. Undaunted by their disappointments in Toronto's church life, they set out the following Sunday morning. The city was bright and modern, much more so than they had expected. The electric street railway made travel exceptionally easy. Not all the downtown streets were paved, but all were readily accessible. Their first hope was to find a Methodist Church where they would feel at home. If that failed, they would seek a Baptist Church, with the hope of finding one with a similar personality to Velma's home church in Moncton.

So thinking, they set out shortly after 8:30 on Sunday morning, October 22nd, to catch the streetcar on First Street. It turned out to be the day that changed their lives forever.

While Henry and Velma were waiting, dressed in their finest Sunday clothes, two ladies approached, also dressed for church. Each carried a large handbag (the style from two years earlier, at least in Moncton). Each wore a large, veiled hat (also dated), with an appropriately large hatpin, and each carried a large black Bible.

Despite their somewhat unusual appearance (at least to the newcomers) they were cheerful and outgoing. They laughed and talked brightly and enthusiastically, as if going to church was the greatest joy and delight in their lives. Velma was immediately drawn to them. It had been a long time since she had seen people so clearly enjoying the prospect of being on their way to worship. It reminded her of her own childhood in Moncton when her mother would meet her friends going into church and visit with the same relaxed good cheer. Her heart leapt.   Both women greeted Velma and Henry warmly, expressing thankfulness to the Lord for the warmth and sunshine, and for the blessing of "Sabbath worship." Velma and Henry returned the greeting just as warmly and introduced themselves.

Miss Tilley, the senior of the group, asked Velma where they were going to church.

Velma's response seemed to be the one expected, for Miss Tilley's reply was instant:

"You haven't found one yet? Well Lord bless you, isn't that providential! You must come with us! We're just getting started in our little church and we need all the help we can get. Why, I was just saying to Miss Foster here, as we walked up to the car stop, how the Lord promised me we'd have some new folks in church this morning."

Velma, a little overwhelmed at their openness and enthusiasm, so uncharacteristic of her New Brunswick roots, sputtered a grateful, yet somewhat embarrassed assent. Henry, a little more at ease with the familiarity on short notice from his contact with his Prince Edward Island relatives, smiled sheepishly but with simple enthusiasm. It was settled on the spot.

It never occurred to either Henry or Velma to ask what kind of church it might be. They were just happy to have met friends who would make them feel welcome.

As they rode the streetcar heading west, to where, they didn't know, Miss Tilley continued chatting brightly while the others were content to listen.

"I've been praying for the service this morning for weeks. We have a visiting preacher from California, of all places. He's just here for this Sunday, unless the Lord lays it on his heart to stay longer. We don't have anyone to play the organ yet, so it's hard to have a good song service. Without good singing, it's hard to get the glory down! That's what Brother Brown said last month when he was down from Edmonton to organize the church."

She paused for a breath. The streetcar clanged over a rough intersection and the sparks flew as the electricity arced when the contact pole momentarily lost contact at the intersection of wires.

The smell of ozone touched Velma's nostrils, startling her, yet reminding her of the fresh smell after a Moncton thunderstorm.

In the momentary lull, Miss Tilley looked at Velma's hands. Though they were sheathed in long white gloves, Velma's long, elegant fingers struck her with a thought:

"You play, don't you? Ain't the Lord good! He wouldn't give you hands like those without givin' you a gift to use them for! The Lord be praised!"

Velma and Henry were both shocked that this stranger could know, just from the look of her hands, that Velma did play the organ and had for years.

"Why, yes," said Velma, cautiously, "I do play. Only hymns and gospel songs, though," she added, somewhat irrelevantly.

"You will play for us this morning, then," added Miss Foster with enthusiasm equal to Miss Tilley's. "Oh, please say that you will. You're such an answer to prayer."

Velma was not as quick to acknowledge it openly, but in her heart she knew that these simple elderly spinsters were, too, an answer to her prayers. She hadn't stepped inside the church yet but already she knew she had found the church where she and Henry belonged.

Velma wrote to her mother about it when she and Henry returned home that night:

> "You'll never believe the amazing things that happened to us today! We found a church that seems to suit us perfectly. And you'll never believe who the speaker was this morning: It was Rev. Mr. Ashley, who used to be the pastor at Central Methodist Church right there in Moncton. Remember how he moved away to California because of some disagreement with the Bishop?

Well he's with a new church now. They call themselves the Church of the Nazarene, and they have a congregation here in Calgary. O, Mother, you would just love it. They sing all the songs we used to sing in the parlour at home. They asked me to play the organ, as they don't have many members yet. They even had Henry help in taking up the offering.

Mr. Ashley remembered Henry right away, as soon as Henry told him who he was. He asked about Henry's father. He hadn't heard about his death. He was so sympathetic when Henry told him all about it. He even assured him that God understands the sorrow that poor Walter went through. It was the first word of hope that Henry has ever heard since the poor man's death. It was like a new breath of spiritual life for Henry.

We spent the whole day at church! And loved every minute of it! The pastor, Mr. Bell made us feel we were wanted and needed here. The people are so friendly and so enthusiastic. I don't know much about this Church of the Nazarene yet but I do know they're the kind of people I want to be around."

Velma's letter went on for several more pages, informing her mother of every detail of their new life here on the prairies. There were no tears this time as she sealed the letter and addressed it for mailing. For the first time since they'd left Moncton they felt completely at home. And for Henry, it was the first time since his mother had died that he felt at home and comfortable in Church.

II

HENRY STARTED DRINKING the following spring. Velma was worried one Friday evening in late March when Henry didn't arrive home at the usual time. It was so odd for Henry to be late that Velma was inclined to believe the worst; that there had been an accident at the railyard. An hour passed, then two. She was just at the point of becoming frantic when she heard the front door open and Henry's footsteps on the stairway. She breathed a prayer of thanks, but when he stumbled coming through the apartment door her joy was abruptly ended. She knew right away!

Henry's explanation was brief. The shop foreman had been promoted to shop superintendent that very day. He had asked Henry to come into his office just after the announcement was made.

"Henry," he had said, "I've been watching you since you started here last fall. You are the best worker in the plant. You are the most mature man, too, in your ability to lead the others. I have to select someone to be foreman and you're my choice.

"There's just one thing I would say to you before I make the announcement. You're going to have to get closer to the men. They like you and respect you, but some of them think you're too much of a loner. You never stop off for a drink with them after work. You keep too much to yourself during lunch breaks. Some of them even say you read your Bible while they're playing cards at lunch.

"What you do is your own business, of course. I admire independence as much as anyone does. But if you're going to make it as a leader, you'll have to get to know them. You'll have to show them that they can trust you."

Velma was heartsick as she listened to Henry's slurred explanation. She protested that one of the things they had agreed on before their marriage was that they would never use alcohol and would never allow it to be part of their life. Henry's response was that they had only been children when they agreed on that. Besides, he went on, the Methodist Church they visited in Toronto had taken its stand on moderation, not total abstinence. It wouldn't be a problem!

It wasn't a big problem at first, at least from Henry's point of view. Velma came to dread Fridays. Henry, true to his word, never came home drunk again, but was always an hour or so later than on other nights. No matter how often he explained to Velma that he didn't like it any more than she did, that it was just company policy and he was actually getting closer to the men, and that some of the men had even started to ask questions about his church, Velma worried. The image of drunken Walter Adams' dead body being dragged from the mud below the Gunningsville Bridge haunted her. It didn't help, either, that Henry, as he matured was looking more and more like his father.

No one at the church ever made an issue of it, though they couldn't help but know. The church was growing quickly and many of the newcomers were rail workers. Sometimes during the services, especially when Brother Bell preached about entire sanctification, Velma would sense that Henry was feeling uneasy. She would glance sideways at him, hoping to get some indication that the message was getting through to him, but she noticed no movement.

Finally, one Sunday night as the invitation to seek entire sanctification was given, Velma realized for the first time that tonight, the message was for her, not for Henry. Her letter to her mother later that week described what happened. After her usual newsy correspondence about everything interesting and exciting in her life, Velma wrote:

> "... It was as if God was speaking directly to me. Mother, I never felt anything like it before. I remember how I felt the moment I knew I was saved. This

was something like that but different too. When I got saved I felt such a weight of responsibility descend upon me. I was just a little girl but I felt then as if I had to be perfect to please God and that He would be watching me every moment.

It wasn't a bad feeling for a little girl but it got to be bad later. The constant feeling that I was never good enough, that God was always unhappy with me no matter how hard I tried, seemed to grow as I grew older. It got so I welcomed the rituals and ceremonies at church because they distracted me from what I feared God might be saying to me.

Mom, tonight all that changed! I have never felt so free before! I don't understand the doctrine of entire sanctification very well, I'm sure! But I know that when I asked God for it, whatever "it" is, something changed inside me and I actually wanted to be as close to God as I can get! I don't want to keep Him as far away as possible and still stay in touch. Ever since that experience I want to keep Him near me.

The most amazing thing, Mom, was to discover what I had been unwilling to surrender to God. Henry's drinking! When God asked me to leave that to Him, my answer was, "No!" We fought it out (God and me, not Henry and me) for ever so long. I finally saw that my unwillingness to let go of it was keeping me from perfect fellowship with God. When I did let go, it was as if God's Spirit moved right inside me.

When I described it to the people after the service, Pastor Bell said that is one of the ways of explaining what happens at entire sanctification: "the in-filling of the Spirit." I don't know how else to describe it for you but I have had spiritual peace and joy ever since.

Henry hasn't stopped drinking but it has stopped troubling me the way it was. I'm still concerned, mind you, but it's not preoccupying me and keeping me defeated. I know — it seems to me that God has promised it — that He will take care of it in the right time. For right now it's enough to recognize that Henry has kept his promise to not get drunk."

Velma's letter went on for several pages. Her newfound experience with God gave her a joy she never had felt before. She couldn't wait for next Sunday! She finished her letter with a "post script":

"By the way," she added coyly, "the baby is due sometime around the first of June."

III

HENRY'S WORLD COLLAPSED for a second time when on May 31st Velma went into labour. It was Friday and she was in agony when Henry came in from work as customary, one hour later than on other nights. He rushed her to the hospital praying desperately for God's and her forgiveness for keeping her waiting while he had his beer with the boys from work.

Two hours later, an ashen-faced doctor came to the waiting room to tell Henry the bad news. They hadn't been able to save the baby, a little boy; Velma was unconscious, struggling for her own life. The outcome was uncertain.

A flood of memories overwhelmed Henry as he recalled the despair he and his father had gone through seventeen years earlier when the same thing had occurred to Henry's mother. The doctor told him there was nothing left to do but wait. Henry asked if he could see Velma, but the answer was that it would be better for her if she wasn't disturbed.

"Come back tomorrow," was the last the doctor would say.

At home, Henry paced the floor sleeplessly. He knew he had to work in the morning but didn't know how he could. Shortly before midnight he thought of Pastor Bell. He telephoned to the pastor's home but there was no answer. He thought of Velma's dear friends, Sisters Tilley and Foster, but they didn't have a telephone. There were others in the church that he could have called, but in his despair all he could think of was Velma suffering alone in the hospital bed.

Shortly after one o'clock he made his way quietly to the cellar below the apartment building, to the secret storage place he had made. He had promised Velma he would never bring liquor into their home, but tonight was different. Without her there, it was no longer their home. It was like a strange, alien territory. He reached up, found the quart bottle he had won in the betting pool at work. He took it and crept up the dark stairway, back up to the lonely apartment, and an hour later drinking was no longer "not a problem" to Henry.

Early in the evening of June 1st, pastor Bell arrived, unannounced but very welcome, at Henry's door. Henry was just in from work and had not eaten but had already finished his first double shot of whiskey. Mr. Bell's genuine pastoral sympathy, his willingness to stay and pray, despite Henry's impairment, had a double effect on Henry. He was truly thankful for a pastor who cared, but overwhelmed with guilt at his own weakness. For a while the guilt won out.

Velma was in the hospital for six weeks. She recovered, but slowly and sadly, especially as she noticed what was happening to Henry. He came to see her every evening as soon as work was done. Even on Friday night he was punctual, no visit to the bar with the boys. But she could see that while she was sustained in her sadness by her Lord, Henry was wrestling with ghosts from the distant past.

By the second week she realized that, though he didn't go drinking with the boys after work, a worse scenario was developing: he was drinking heavily at home, filling his emptiness with the only consolation he would accept.

Pastor Bell came to see him again, the week before Velma came home from the hospital. He was as compassionate as always, but seemed troubled. He finally got to the point. God was calling him to serve elsewhere. He hated to leave this young and thriving congregation, but the Divine imperative was clear: his job was to plant; another would come to nurture the congregation to maturity.

Before he left that evening, Pastor Bell spoke earnestly to Henry about his sorrow and the consequent drinking.

"Henry," he began, "God has great things for you and Velma in the future. He needs you to become strong and courageous through this sorrow. God didn't cause it and you didn't cause it; and it's certain that your father didn't cause it. Velma told me the whole story of what happened when you were a child. I can see why you have reacted the way you have. But just as you needed your father to be strong then, Velma needs you to be strong now.

"Sorrow," he continued, "can either drive you closer to God or away from Him. You need to choose! You're free, as your father was, to try to find your comfort in a bottle, and in so doing destroy yourself and harm all those who love you; or you can find your comfort in the Lord. He is giving Velma back to you. She's getting stronger every day. But she needs you to be strong, too. Will you?"

Henry promised to try. Pastor Bell asked him to do one thing for him before he left. Henry assumed that would be to quit drinking. To his amazement that was not what Pastor Bell asked.

"Doctor Bresee will be arriving on the train on the evening of July 22, to conduct our District Assembly. Would you be willing to meet him at the station and bring him to the church for me? He comes in on the 6:43 train from Vancouver, and I need to be at the church by then. It would mean a lot to me if you would take care of it."

"Of course I would," stammered Henry, overwhelmed at the honour and the responsibility committed to him, especially given his present situation. After Pastor Bell prayed and left, Henry vowed he would never drink again.

He made it through that night but the next evening the sadness returned and before he realized it he had downed two more double shots of whiskey. Two led to more and by the time he slipped tearfully into sleep he had finished another bottle. The last thing he remembered that night was praying again that God would make him strong enough to quit this awful habit that so quickly had taken possession of him.

Velma came home the following Monday, July 9th, weakened but thankful to be alive. Henry hid his new bottle in the cellar again, praying that he would have the strength never to retrieve it. Every evening he thought of it, but resisted the temptation. Friday night came: he resisted the bottle in the cellar, but substituted his old habit of stopping off with the boys after work.

Velma didn't scold or find fault. She renewed her commitment to "let go and let God take care of it" as was so often advised in their church. For two weeks life returned to its old pattern, now bittersweet because of their recent visitation of sorrow.

IV

MONDAY, JULY 22ND, 1912 proved to be a turning point in Henry's life. By the weekend he realized he would never again be the same person as he had been.

When Henry arrived on Monday night with Dr. Bresee, the small church — nothing more than a converted one-room schoolhouse on Fourteenth Street West — was packed, as the saying went, to the rafters. The singing had already begun, with Mrs. Milton Williams at the piano. Her husband, the Rev. L. Milton Williams was scheduled to preach that evening. Dr. Bresee, in his advancing years, preferred not to preach at assembly opening services. Velma, in her still delicate condition, was not able to attend, so her place at the organ was filled by Mrs. H. D. Brown, the wife of the District Superintendent.

As Henry and Dr. Bresee approached the front of the church, Bresee smiled warmly at Henry and said,

"Do you hear that singing? They've got the glory down! This is going to be a great Assembly!"

It was Wednesday night, though, when it happened to Henry. Each time they had met through the week, Henry had listened intently to this gentle, yet fiery preacher, who had so quietly assumed the best about him. Bresee had talked with Henry as if Jesus was his best friend, and as if he just assumed he was Henry's best friend, too. There was no pretense, no pomp or ceremony about him. He merely glowed with a warmth that attracted everyone.

Henry was intent on discovering what the secret was, what made this man so different from so many other preachers he had met. He listened to every word, hungering for a clue to his strange combination of intensity and serenity. Velma, against Henry's better judgment, had decided she was well enough to attend this one service. The "glory was down" again and by the time Dr. Bresee rose to preach, there was a level of expectancy which Henry had never experienced in a church service.

The text was short, but to the point. Rev. L. Milton Williams read the scripture passage from Matthew 11:28-30: "Come unto me, all ye that labour and are heavy laden, and I will give you rest. Take my yoke upon you, and learn of me; for I am meek and lowly in heart: and ye shall find rest unto your souls. For my yoke is easy, and my burden is light."

Dr. Bresee chose as his text, the promise, "you shall find rest unto your souls." As Dr. Bresee preached, Henry sensed progressively, a hungering for that promised "soul rest," a self-revelation at the things he personally had tried to attain that rest, a despairing that it ever could be attained, and finally a revival of hope as the promise was again renewed. He looked back through the tattered pages of his life and saw clearly, for the first time, the angry rebellion against God that seethed just below the surface in his soul.

When the gentle, yet insistent invitation was given to "come to that rest," Henry knew immediately that what was being offered was what he needed. That "rest" filled his heart, not after a long struggle at the altar-rail, but at the moment he took his first step toward the place of prayer.

As he reached the front, Dr. Bresee extended his hand to Henry and said, "I see you have found it! Don't let anyone or anything ever take it from you. It's a pearl of great price, bought with the blood of Jesus. He has promised it to you forever if you will cherish it above all else. Keep the glory down in your life."

The next morning, as Dr. Bresee said goodbye to Henry and Velma at the station, he took Henry aside for a moment and said,

> *"We won't meet again this side of Heaven. I only have a few more days to labour before the Lord calls me home. I need to tell you something that the Lord*

has laid on my heart. You feel sorrow and sadness very deeply, young man. That is both a blessing and a curse. If you continue to commit that tenderness to the Lord and let him continue to sanctify it, you will prove to be a blessing to others all your life. If you let it run wild, it will destroy you and everyone you love. Let His Spirit fill you daily and He will keep His glory in your life. Do that and I'll meet you in heaven, without any doubt: When you get there, look for me; I'll be waiting just inside the Eastern Gate."

Henry had only a moment to make the promise that he would. The train came, was gone, and Henry never saw Dr. Bresee again in this world. He never forgot his promise to Dr. Bresee but more importantly, he never forgot the "rest for his soul," which God had given to him the night before. He never was the same again.

V

THE REMAINDER OF that summer, as Velma regained her strength, she and Henry availed themselves of every opportunity to learn more about this life of total surrender to God. They made an effort to attend every tent meeting within driving distance.

Henry would get home as early as possible after work on Friday night and they would drive in their second-hand Ford to places like Stettler, Drumheller, Wetaskiwin, and even as far away as Red Deer to hear the holiness message proclaimed and explained. Although the explanations never measured up to the experience, they gradually came to understand something of the significance and meaning of what God had done for them. On the return trip, often the same evening, or sometimes on Saturday night, they would discuss what they had learned and marvel at God's goodness to them.

Almost without exception they would be home for Sunday to fill their place in Calgary First Church, as it had come to be known. With all the enthusiasm they felt for the excitement of the camp meeting environment, they knew the real work of the church was done at the home church.

One of the rare exceptions was the trip they made in early September that year. The Company sent Henry to Saskatoon for a week-long series of meetings. Velma accompanied him on the train for Henry didn't like to leave her alone even yet. At the station they noticed a handbill posted on one of the walls announcing the Saskatoon Holiness Convention. The services were being conducted that entire week with Rev. Augustus Ashley as preacher and Dr. Charles Thompson as musician.

Henry and Velma were both anxious to see Pastor Ashley and tell him what God had done for them. They made plans to attend as many of the services as Henry's work schedule would permit. The first session they were able to attend was on Saturday night.

When they walked in, Pastor Bell and Pastor Ashley were greeting people at the back of the auditorium. Both pastors welcomed them warmly, and introduced them to a few other people. They were just ready to take their seats when Henry caught sight of someone he recognized on the far side of the convention hall.

He drew Velma with him and they made their way through the crowded room. As they approached, there could be no mistake. It was Gordon and Bertha Lister, acquaintances from Moncton. Gordon had been one of the foremen at the repair shops when Henry had started work there. He had "gone west" a couple of years later, and Henry had never given him another thought.

Following the service they got reacquainted. Velma and Bertha hit it off immediately and became lifelong friends. All four shared the excitement of their newfound religious experience and their interest in pursuing holiness. Henry and Gordon had a common interest in bringing the Gospel to children: Velma and Bertha, in the deeper life. When they parted later that evening, it was with fond anticipation of corresponding and building their friendship.

VI

FOR HENRY AND Velma the following years were the mixture of joy and sadness that is the common human lot. Their disappointment at not being able to have children drove them to, rather than from, their Lord. It never became a source of bitterness. He blessed their love for children with opportunities beyond measure in Sunday School, summer camps, and daily life. Their childlessness freed them to invest their lives wholeheartedly in working with all children, wherever they met them.

Henry soon became assistant Sunday School superintendent at Calgary First Church, with special responsibility for outreach to un-churched children. He arranged for teaching Sunday School classes in homes, at the public school, and in Eagle Hall over on First Street West where the church met before they bought their own building. Henry was completely at home working with children! He felt their hurts with them, anticipated their needs, and knew just how to point them to Jesus at exactly the right moment.

When he became aware that many of the children he met were immigrants, unable to understand the English language, he sought-out and recruited people of other languages to assist them. As Dr. Bresee had just assumed the best about him, he found it easy to assume the best about others: in reaching out to them, asking for their help, and trusting them. many of these tutors found the Lord.

The news that they would never have children of their own was the occasion of another milestone for Henry and Velma. Velma decided in the fall of 1912 to enroll in the Normal School, over on Fourth Avenue, and prepare to be a public school teacher. When she began her duties teaching grade three at Central School the following year, she wrote home to her mother,

> ". . . Besides that, the school is beautiful! There is a separate class for each grade level, and some of the younger grades actually need two classes. The population is growing so quickly, both from the birth rate and the immigration rate. There are children everywhere! I have fifty-three students, though there are only forty desks in the class. The other grade three class has fifty-one students, and they, too, have only forty desks. The principal would start a third class immediately if he had a teacher and a classroom.
>
> Oh, Mother! You and Dad should come to Calgary! You could teach school, too; and Henry is desperate for good workers. Dad could work for him! Since he became foreman he has seen how hard it is to recruit good skilled help. Dad could make a hundred and twenty dollars a month here! And I know you could make eighty-five dollars a month teaching. Please pray about it! Please!

VII

VELMA'S PARENTS DIDN'T take her up on her officer but by 1917 Henry had traveled, first with District Superintendent W.B. Tait, and later with Tait's successor, James H. Bury, to Edmonton, Red Deer, Claresholm, Rimbey, and Camrose, helping to organize and establish Sunday Schools and a corps of children's workers. His energy and enthusiasm, coupled with his total implacability, proved contagious, fuelling cooperation and growth wherever he went.

In later years, he and Velma would say that though their childlessness was a cross to bear, it gave them a freedom to be spiritual parents to hundreds of children they would otherwise have never known. They were "at rest" in the work the Lord gave them to do.

In 1921, Henry was promoted to superintendent of the Calgary engine repair shop and in 1930, while thousands were unemployed; he became general manager of all repair operations for Western Canada. The new responsibilities, which included extensive travel throughout all of Western Canada, while curtailing his local children's ministry, gave him occasion to visit and encourage new Nazarene Churches and Sunday Schools as they sprung up in dozens of communities in all the western provinces.

Toronto 1944

I

THE PAINS HAD started just after they passed through Cochrane Ontario, but Henry said nothing to Velma. He didn't want to worry her; besides, what could she do about it anyway? On the train you just had to wait until you arrived at your destination to receive medical care. By the time they had passed the depot at Parry Sound, Henry could no longer hide the fact that something was dreadfully wrong. His face was ashen as he tried to get to his feet in their bedroom compartment. Velma saw the distress he was in and jumped to assist him. She knew immediately that he shouldn't be standing and helped him over to the bed. His voice was barely audible as he struggled to ask for a glass of water.

Velma rang immediately for the cabin steward and then drew a tumbler of water from the tap at the sink. She searched desperately through her purse for the bottle of aspirin that she always carried. After emptying everything out of her purse onto the table, she remembered that she had put them in her suitcase. Quickly she gave two to Henry, then, sensing the depth of his distress, she gave him two more. In a few minutes his breathing seemed easier and his voice returned almost to normal.

After an hour, when the steward had still not arrived, she rang again. Another hour had passed and the express train had rumbled through Barrie before he finally arrived. He apologized for responding so slowly but reminded Velma of the war effort that left the railroad very short staffed. Henry was sleeping fitfully by now, but Velma didn't like his color.

"We need to get him to a hospital as quickly as possible," she pled to the steward. "I'm sure it's his heart. We don't have any time to lose."

"I'll check the passenger list and see if there is a doctor aboard," the steward offered. "If there is, perhaps he could help until we get to Toronto. We'll be at Union Station in eighty-seven minutes," he said, looking at his watch.

"Could we stop the train and go back to Barrie?" Velma asked in desperation. "There must be a hospital there."

"There's an express freight train on this line just forty minutes behind us," was the response. "It would be impossible to get stopped and back-up to a siding on time to let it past. Besides, even if we were successful, we would lose more time than pressing on to Toronto. I'll ask the conductor if we can move any faster, but we're pretty close to the limit now."

There was no doctor on board but they were able to gain four and one half minutes, arriving at Union Station at 4:47 PM. The steward had sent for a porter who was ready to help Henry and Velma to the platform the moment the train stopped.

As they stepped down from the coach, they were overwhelmed, as they had been thirty-four years earlier, with the size, the noise, and the speed of everything. The platform was crowded with soldiers rushing to get their suitcases and footlockers. Those arriving were being mobbed by mothers, wives, and children, all shrieking and weeping for joy; those departing were repressing tears, lingering in long embraces and finally drawing away reluctantly to mount the steps to the coaches. There were businessmen in sharply tailored suits, and sad, foreign-speaking immigrants who looked as bewildered as Velma felt.

She had no idea what to do next. The porter who had been so helpful on the train had disappeared back into the recesses of the dark train passageway. Other porters were busy responding to the loudest and most demanding voices in the horde of new arrivals. Henry leaned heavily on Velma's arm for support. The pain had returned, full force, and his face was turning gray. Velma looked frantically around, unsure even of which direction to go. She whispered a prayer, "Lord Jesus, send someone to help!"

That very moment, a tall young man who had just arrived on another train, glanced at her. He was talking and laughing with three companions who had just disembarked the train on track four. He seemed to sense her distress and leaving his friends, strode quickly to her side.

"Good evening ma'am," he said, in a smooth, rich, warm voice. "My name is Charles Templeton. You seem to be having trouble. Is there anything I can do to help you?"

Until her dying day, Velma vowed that those words spoken were like the voice of Jesus Himself to her. She quickly poured out the story of her plight to him. She had to get Henry to a hospital immediately or she feared he would die right there on the platform.

The young man called to his companions:

"Billy! Bev! Cliff! Could you come over here? These folks need help. Connie will be waiting with the car on Front Street. Why don't you help me get them to the car."

The three companions strode quickly over. Billy, the tallest, with a shock of unruly blond hair and the most engaging smile imaginable, picked up the three suitcases the porter had deposited beside Henry and Velma. The other two went, one to each side of Henry's sagging body.

Moments later, they stepped into the late-afternoon sunshine of Front Street where a black-haired, black-eyed young woman was waiting in a burgundy and tan McLaughlin-Buick.

As they loaded the luggage into the trunk and helped Henry into the back seat, Mr. Templeton quickly gave his instructions:

"You three can leave your bags here in the car. Just take what you need for the service tonight and catch a cab to Varsity Arena. Torrey will meet you at the College Street entrance. He was on the same train from Chicago as we were, so he should get there about the same time you do. Connie and I will take Mr. and Mrs. Adams over to St. Michael's hospital on Queen Street. I'll stay with them as long as I need to and make sure they are settled."

"But Chuck," Billy protested in his musical southern drawl, "you're scheduled to preach tonight. And Connie is scheduled to sing. All the handbills and posters have people looking forward to it. I hate to disappoint them."

"We'll get there as soon as we can. If we aren't there on time, have Bev sing that one he sang last night at Chicago Stadium. And Billy, you can preach if I don't get there. You've never disappointed a crowd. Just tell Torrey Johnson that I'm doing what he taught us; being open to the Lord's leading."

With that he jumped into the front seat, leaving Billy, George and Cliff standing there, and he told Connie to drive to St. Michael's.

"Mr. Templeton, you're a preacher?" Velma said in amazement. "You're supposed to preach tonight but you've changed your plans in order to help us? I don't know what to say; I mean, I don't know how to thank you!"

"I guess I just believe that this is what Jesus would do if he were here. Billy is a great preacher. The Youth for Christ rally will go fine without me if I don't get there tonight. The Lord takes care of every detail."

Somehow they were able to negotiate the traffic and pull into the emergency entrance to the hospital in just over three minutes. In ten minutes they had Henry on a gurney and several attendants wheeled him away to another room.

"The situation looks grave," was the only comment the doctor would make. An hour later, after the admission process was completed, Velma sat with Chuck and Connie Templeton in the waiting area outside the treatment room where they had taken Henry. It was the first time they had an opportunity to exchange any information other than the barest necessities.

"Do you have family here in Toronto?" asked Connie.

"No," replied Velma. "We were just passing through on our way back home to Moncton. Henry's heart has been a problem for the last two or three years. We decided that he should retire from the railroad in Calgary and we should go back home."

"New Brunswick!" exclaimed Chuck. "We have a lot of people in our congregation from New Brunswick; in fact, we have people from all over the Maritimes."

"You are a pastor?" inquired Velma.

"Oh yes," replied Chuck, "a pastor and an evangelist. I am the pastor at the Avenue Road Church of the Nazarene, but I'm also the evangelist for Youth for Christ in Canada. The other men you met are from Youth for Christ in Chicago."

"Henry and I are members of the Church of the Nazarene in Calgary. Calgary First Church," Velma offered. "Isn't it marvellous how God sent you to meet our need there at the station? If you hadn't come along the very moment I prayed for help, we'd still be there on the platform. I can't praise the Lord enough or thank you enough."

"Let's pray together again and then Connie and I need to get over to the arena for the service. I'll find someone from the church that you can stay with for a few days, if you wish. When Mr. Adams is well enough to travel, we will see that you get back to the station and safely on your way. We'll come back here after the service.

II

IT WAS A few minutes before midnight when Chuck arrived back at the hospital. The nurses had tried to insist that Velma leave when visiting hours ended at eight-thirty. She had resolutely, but sweetly, refused to go. She sat on a straight back chair in the hallway, just outside the ward where Henry lay.

As Chuck approached, a grim-faced doctor stepped through the door and spoke to Velma. Henry's situation had deteriorated. He was conscious and asking for her. Chuck escorted her into the room and stood quietly at the foot of the bed while Velma went to Henry's side.

After a few moments of quiet conversation Velma asked, "Would you like to have Mr. Templeton pray with you?" Henry nodded weakly.

Chuck stepped to the other side of the bed opposite Velma. Henry beckoned for him to bend low over the bed. The movement of his hand left him weaker. Tears welled up in Velma's eyes as Henry waited for strength to speak. When he had caught his breath he asked,

"Would you mind reading a few verses from Matthew 11? That's what Dr. Bresee preached from the night I got sanctified back in 1912. I'd like to be able to remember every detail of that service but I only remember the verse he spoke from and what he said as he was leaving the building that night."

"Which verse was it?" asked Chuck.

"It was the part about finding rest for your soul. You go ahead and read and I'll stop you when you come to it," responded Henry.

"Come unto me all ye who labour and are heavy laden," began Chuck, "and I will give you rest. Take my yoke upon you and learn of me, for I am meek and lowly in heart. And ye shall find rest unto your souls."

When he came to the words, "ye shall find rest unto your souls," Henry stopped him.

"That's it! That's the promise! I've read it again and again over the years since that night in 1912 but it's always better when someone else reads it," he said weakly. "I'm going to that eternal rest tonight. Another place in the scripture says that Jesus has gone to prepare a place for me. He's had thirty-two years to work on it; I guess it should be ready by now."

"Oh, Henry," Velma sobbed, "don't leave me now, not here in this strange place. Try to hold on, try to get better so we can get settled back in Moncton."

"It's not my choice to make, dearest," he returned. "Jesus is calling me, just as He did that night back in 1912. I have to go to Him. Remember where He said to His disciples, 'Let not your heart be troubled.' It was the night before He died. It's meant for you tonight. Jesus will take care of you better than I've ever done. Just trust Him. It will all work out."

Henry's voice had grown faint again as he struggled for his next breath. Into the silence, broken only by Henry's laboured gasps for breath, Chuck began to read again, this time from John 14. When he got to the words, "I am the Way, the Truth and the Life. No man cometh unto the Father but by me," Henry was peaceful once more.

He spoke one last time:

"As he was leaving that night, Mr. Bresee said the other thing I remember. It was kind of a slogan to him, I found out later, but it really helped me that night. Going out the door of old Calgary First Church he grasped my hand and asked, 'Do you have victory in your heart, brother?' I answered, 'Yes sir. Jesus has given me rest for my soul.' With a twinkle in his eye that I'll see again in a few minutes he said, 'I'll meet you in the resurrection morning. I'll be waiting just inside the Eastern Gate.' Then he was out the door.

"He repeated that part of it the next morning at the station, when we said goodbye. It seemed so strange then, so distant and unreal. It's real now! Velma: promise me when your time comes that you'll meet me there too."

Those were his last words. Velma, through her tears, managed to say, "You know I'll be there Henry. I love you!" Henry grimaced in one last spasm of pain, then a smile covered his face as he slipped away to be with Jesus.

"Could I pray for you?" Chuck asked.

"Yes, Mr. Templeton, please do," Velma agreed.

In his smooth, rich voice, Chuck began: "Lord Jesus, you stood at the grave of your friend Lazarus and wept because you felt then what we feel now. Receive this good man Henry unto yourself as you promised you would. Draw close to his wife and loved ones that, through this time of sorrow, they will see their faith in you grow stronger. Comfort them, I pray, that they too, when their time comes, will pass into everlasting blessedness. Amen."

Velma repeated the "Amen," and Chuck went to call a nurse.

III

VELMA WENT TO stay that night at the home of a young widow from Avenue Road Church. Ruth Currie had lost her husband suddenly a few months before. He, like Henry, had died suddenly from a heart attack but unlike Velma, Ruth was left with three children; two young boys and a girl.

knowing her gift for hospitality, Pastor Templeton had telephoned Mrs. Currie from the stadium. He would normally have called his mother, the elder Mrs. Templeton, in this kind of circumstance, but she had been quite ill recently. Mrs. Currie was glad to accommodate the request from her beloved pastor.

Chuck and Connie drove the heartbroken Velma from the hospital, up Yonge Street to Roxborough Avenue and turned left. At Avenue Road, they passed a large stone and brick church whose sign boldly proclaimed, "Avenue Road Church of the Nazarene — Pastor C. B. Templeton." They turned right on Avenue Road and went a short block to Dupont Street. Four houses in, on the left, they pulled over to the curb. "We're here," said Connie gently.

Although it was after 1:00 a.m., Mrs. Currie was waiting up with lights on and the kettle boiling. She welcomed her guest, bade goodbye to the Templetons after another prayer, and ushered Velma into the cozy parlour. After her long day and her distressing evening at the hospital, Velma was ready for a cup of tea and the plate of doughnuts that Mrs. Currie offered.

When Ruth, as she insisted that Velma call her, showed Velma to a small but comfortable room an hour or so later, they had wept together, prayed together and had become lifetime friends.

The next day, Mr. Templeton was at the door at 8:30 a.m. When he arrived, Mrs. Currie had just rushed Robert, Chuck, and little Janet out the door to school. Velma was again deeply thankful for his thoughtfulness for she hadn't the slightest idea what to do next. Pastor Templeton had it all under control.

He was leaving on the 11:40 a.m. train for a Youth For Christ Rally in Ottawa and had telephoned neighbouring pastor Bob Woods from St. Clair Church to enlist his help for Velma. Mr. and Mrs. Woods took her to St. Michael's hospital at 1:30 that afternoon to claim Henry's body and sign the papers for its release.

Pastor Templeton had already made arrangements with Canadian National Rail to ship the remains to Moncton, subject, of course, to Velma's wishes. He had even called Pastor Layton Tattrie at First Church in Moncton and asked him to meet Velma at the station when she arrived with Henry's body.

The paperwork would be completed for shipping the body late that afternoon. It would be another day before Velma could catch the train to Montreal where she could make her connection to Moncton the following day at 5:15 p.m.

Moncton 1944

I

VELMA'S RETURN TO Moncton after a thirty-three year absence overwhelmed her with waves of nostalgia — that bittersweet mixture of delightful memory and matured sorrow. The last time she had stood on the platform at the Moncton station Henry stood beside her and they were both in the bloom of youth. As she stood there surveying the altered scene before her, she wondered how the years could have so swiftly passed by. The immediate premises of the depot were virtually unaltered but the surrounding city had changed in ways she couldn't immediately identify.

Ignoring the teeming crowds of soldiers, businessmen and other travelers, Velma scanned the horizon for familiar landmarks but few presented themselves. Peering intently to the southeast, she tried to pick out the white spire of First Baptist Church; only after several moments of disorientation did she remember her mother's letter about the fire in 1913, and the subsequent rebuilding of the stone and brick replacement building. She couldn't identify the new church among the several that had been built since her departure.

Glancing back along the train from which she had just disembarked, she saw something she could identify: the pine crate that carried the coffin and the mortal remains of her Henry was being unloaded from one of the baggage cars. The flood of grief she had felt periodically since his death — could it only be four days ago? — swept over her with force amplified by the memories of their youth here in Moncton. She felt faint and grasped a light post to steady herself.

A bright-eyed young couple stepped forward as she clutched the post, leaving a shy looking four-year-old boy standing alone against the station wall.

The woman, obviously in the last weeks of pregnancy, spoke first.

"You must be Mrs. Adams?" she said in a voice as sweet as her countenance predicted. "I'm Mildred Tattrie. This is my husband, Layton. That's our son, Howard, over by the station. Mr. Templeton called to say you would be on this train. We're so sorry to hear of your sorrow. Please let my husband help you."

At this cue, Mr. Tattrie stepped forward and offered his arm to Velma who was recovering from her swoon. Two men approached from the direction of the baggage car, one of whom Velma recognized instantly. It was Gordon Lister, their long-time friend from the west.

Introductions were soon completed and they went into the station house. Bertha Lister rushed immediately to Velma and hugged her tearfully, with many "there-theres" and "dear-dears" and like-words of consolation. The woman with Bertha was introduced to Velma as Alice Marino, wife of Frank, the man who had assisted Gordon in putting the coffin in Tuttle Brothers' hearse. In a moment all were chatting, at ease in the company of mutual faith.

Velma learned that Mrs. Tattrie was likely to go to the hospital at any moment to have her baby and that otherwise, she would have insisted that Velma stay with them. It had been arranged that Velma would stay with the Marinos, as Gordon and Bertha lived in Memramcook, almost thirty miles out of the city.

Mr. Tuttle had taken Henry's remains to the funeral home a few blocks away. They would all go to Marino's home, over on Lefurgy Avenue, for lunch. Then Mr. Tattrie would accompany Velma to the funeral home to make arrangements for the funeral service.

II

THE FOLLOWING THREE weeks, though they unfolded in seeming slow motion, in later years seemed to Velma a blur of frenzied change.

Mr. Tattrie conducted Henry's funeral in the Tuttle Brothers' chapel on Lutz Street because the storefront building on Mountain Road, where the few members of Moncton First Church met from Sunday to Sunday, didn't seem suitable for the congregation's first funeral. The men had begun construction of the new church at the corner of York and Pine streets but it was not even close to usable.

The attendance was small but the Spirit of God was near. Although none of the people attending had known Henry, all of them knew Henry's Saviour, so there was no sense of strangeness. Mr. Tattrie's message was from the text that Henry asked Mr. Templeton to read moments before he died and that Bresee had preached the night Henry had made peace with God, "You will find rest for your soul."

Velma was reconciled to her grief as together the small group pictured Henry's new place of rest in Heaven. When Frances Vine sang "The Eastern Gate" at the close of the service, Velma knew that though the sorrow would not pass in this life, she would be united with Henry again. The peace in her own soul was confirmed.

Velma spent several days revisiting the familiar places of her childhood and young adult years. She walked past the building on

Lester Street where she and Henry had begun their married life. The sense of the proportion of her loss deepened as the memory of past, sweet moments raced through her mind; but equally, the sense of God's goodness deepened too, as she recognized how much she had been given in her life.

She walked past the house on Botsford Street where she had grown up. Everything unimportant was unchanged but everything that might have meant anything was gone. Her father had died in 1931 and her mother now lived in an old-folks home on Princess Street. It broke Velma's heart anew to realize that, though her mother was still technically alive, she no longer knew who she was or where she was. Velma's visits to her were meaningless. Velma went, though, every day and tried to ease the sadness she felt for her many years of absence.

For two weeks Velma followed this routine, vacillating between settling down here and going back to resume her life in Calgary. Her roots were here and she would never be fully severed from them but her life was in Calgary. Her friends, her church, the day-by-day routines and habits, which make life rich were all there, three thousand miles away. But could she go back and pick up the pieces of her life without Henry? She could hardly imagine facing life there without him.

The following Sunday she went with Frank and Alice Marino to the little store-front building on Mountain Road, across from the new High School, and told her new friends of her dilemma. The two-dozen members and friends of Moncton First Church encouraged her to remain there; this new young church needed her and all her experience. They covenanted to pray for the Lord to make His will clear and not to make any firm plans until He had.

Mrs. Tattrie went into the hospital that afternoon and late that evening gave birth to a little boy. On Monday morning when Layton arrived to help the men work on the church building, he was beaming from ear-to-ear. He and his wife had agreed to name the new baby Raymond. Mother and son were doing fine.

When the ladies brought lunch to the workers at noon, everyone, including Velma, was light-hearted. She felt at home among the dear people and felt a real affinity with Pastor and Mrs. Tattrie. She found herself warming to the idea of settling here and making a new life in the remaining years that the Lord would grant her.

On Wednesday, just past midnight, the telephone rang, awakening Velma and the others in the Marino household. She knew from the hushed tones of Alice's conversation that something was dreadfully wrong. It was Pastor Tattrie calling from the hospital.

Mildred had started to haemorrhage unexpectedly shortly before 11:00 p.m. and had died before Layton could get there. His plea was for someone to come and help him. He had no money and no idea what to do next.

Velma thought of her own brush with death under similar circumstances and the effect it had on Henry. She thought, too, of Henry's mother's death and the devastating effect it had on her husband and young child. Her heart was broken for this young pastor and the two little boys he was left to attend. She felt strongly that God had placed her here at this time to offer the comfort that comes only from a soul matured through sorrow.

It was agreed instantly that Alice would go by taxi to Tattrie's apartment to be with little Howard, who was sleeping soundly alone and oblivious to what was happening. (Layton had rushed out immediately when the phone call came, expecting to return shortly.) From there she would call Gordon and Bertha, who would want to know of the tragedy. They would contact the other dozen members of the little church.

Velma insisted that she could go to the hospital alone so that Frank could stay by the phone to receive messages. Frank was content with that arrangement. He hated to go near the hospital over on King Street. The same taxi that would drop Alice off to care for Howard would take Velma to the hospital.

When Velma arrived, a gentle, elderly doctor was trying to explain to Layton what had gone wrong. Layton was weeping uncontrollably, still dripping wet from his run through the rain to get there. As Velma slipped quietly to Layton's side, she thought to herself that she had never seen a more heartbreaking scene. The doctor, assuming that she was Mr. Tattrie's mother, offered his condolences and excused himself to attend to other matters.

Velma remembered the words that Mr. Templeton had prayed for her at Henry's bedside a few days ago and the immediate calming effect they had brought. Gently she touched Mr. Tattrie's arm and asked if she could pray for him.

When she said "Amen," Layton's sobbing had subsided as the Lord's presence settled upon him. The silence that followed was broken only by Layton's deep sighs, and his repeated, bewildered questioning, "O, Lord, what will I do now? What will I ever do now?" Velma had no answer, but had a deep and settled assurance that God would make the way clear for this young preacher.

When they had signed the necessary forms, making arrangements for the funeral home to pick up the body, they returned to Marino's home. From the phone in the kitchen, Velma tried to call Mr. Tink, the district superintendent, to let him know what had happened. When there was no answer she remembered that the Tinks had gone to Eastern Nazarene College in Boston and weren't due back until Saturday. She would try to call them at the college in the morning.

Before they retired for the night they had contacted Mildred's parents, Mr. and Mrs. Charlie Monk, members at St. Clair Church in Toronto. The Monks would leave for Moncton on the train the next morning, arriving late on Friday morning. It was agreed that the funeral should be on Saturday.

When Mr. and Mrs. Tink arrived late Friday night, they had a special guest with them. Velma's phone call had prompted Mr. Tink to call Dr. J. B. Chapman, who was preaching at a revival campaign in New Hampshire. Chapman had insisted that Tink meet him in Dover and bring him to Moncton: he knew in his heart, so he said, that God wanted him there to talk with this brokenhearted young preacher.

So it was that on Saturday afternoon, General Superintendent Chapman preached at Mildred's funeral, assisted by District Superintendent Tink. Tuttle's Funeral Chapel was filled and overflowing, as pastors, and lay people from throughout the Maritimes arrived to comfort and assist in this first major sorrow to directly touch all the people of the fledgling Maritime District of the Church of the Nazarene.

On Sunday morning, Dr. Chapman preached on the death of Jacob's beloved wife Rachel, and how God had used that tragic circumstance to further the plan of salvation.

Following the service, Dr. Chapman took Layton aside to talk with him. "You must face this thing head on," he began, "although you feel like running away. Stay here, and build your church! Let God comfort you in your physical labour, and show these good people of Moncton that what you preach, you also believe. If you run away from this, you'll be running all your life. If you remain, God will see you through and only eternity will reveal the fruits of your faithfulness. God won't let you down."

As Velma overheard this advice, she knew that it was for her, as well as for Mr. Tattrie. She understood immediately the course that she must take. Staying here in Moncton would be running away from her responsibility. It might be comfortable for a while but God still had work for her to do. That work was back in Alberta.

Epilogue

WHEN VELMA DIED in 1968, there was standing room only for the funeral service in Calgary First Church. Tributes flowed in from friends and acquaintances all across Canada.

Nine Nazarene pastors, sent telegrams and phone messages expressing thanks to Velma for paying most of the cost of their educations at Canadian Nazarene College. Some of them were serving churches even smaller than Calgary First had been when she and Henry first attended.

Three missionary families, serving the Lord in distant lands, sent telegrams thanking Velma for the major part she had played in seeing them through the financial pressures of Canadian Nazarene College and Nazarene Theological Seminary.

Three active General Superintendents; Dr. George Coulter, Dr. Edward Lawlor, and Dr. Samuel Young, halted their busy schedules to dictate, over the phone, personal tributes to Velma and appreciation for her personal ministry to them over the years.

The presidents of three Nazarene Colleges, Dr. Arnold Airhart of Canadian Nazarene College, Dr. Edward Mann of Eastern Nazarene College, and Dr. Harold Reed of Olivet Nazarene College, each sent expressions of thanks on behalf of their respective Boards of Governors, for substantial gifts and endowments given by Velma over the years, to assist young men and women preparing for the ministry.

In scores of Nazarene churches from one coast of Canada to the other, hundreds of Nazarenes, most of whom had never met either Henry or Velma, paused to give thanks to God for Velma Adams and thousands of others like her, who had found in The Lowly Nazarene and in the Church which bears his identity, the peace that passes understanding.

Velma had left instructions to have her body shipped to Moncton and buried beside her beloved husband in Elmwood Cemetery. When those instructions were finally carried out, the week after the funeral in Calgary, District Superintendent Robert Woods presided at memorial service in Moncton First Church, assisted by Pastor David Morrison. Mr. Woods recalled the circumstances twenty-five years earlier when he had met Velma, so briefly in Toronto at the time of Henry's death.

Pastor Layton Tattrie, then the pastor of the Church of the Nazarene in Truro, Nova Scotia, spoke briefly at the graveside. He recalled the prayer Velma had prayed that dark night at the old Moncton hospital, when he had lost the dearest person in his young life, and the strength he drew from the faith of this dear, now departed, saint.

After the benediction, as the casket was lowered into its final resting place, those who had gathered joined in singing the hymn, which Henry and Velma had claimed as their theme decades before. It was a fitting remembrance.

> *When peace like a river attendeth my way*
> *When sorrows like sea billows roll:*
> *Whatever my lot, Thou hast taught me to say*
> *It is well, it is well with my soul.*
> Horatio Spafford

Printed in Canada